DATE DUE			
DEC 18			
JAN 21			
NOV 23			
MAY 11			
JAN 30			
NOV 14			

947
JAC

Jacobsen, Karen.

The Soviet Union.

947
JAC

865229 00995   03145A

A New True Book

THE SOVIET UNION

By Karen Jacobsen

Flag of The Soviet Union

CHILDRENS PRESS®
CHICAGO

The Kremlin, an ancient fortress in Moscow,
is the headquarters of the Soviet government.

PHOTO CREDITS

The Bettmann Archive, Inc.—28 (2 photos), 29

Reprinted with permission of *The New Book of Knowledge*, 1989 edition, © Grolier Inc.—5

H. Armstrong Roberts—© L. S. Williams, 25

Hillstrom Stock Photo—© Mary Ann Brockman, 6 (bottom right), 10 (bottom)

Historical Pictures Service, Chicago—22, 26 (left)

© Jason Lauré—45 (bottom left & bottom right)

North Wind Picture Archives—21

Photri—2, 12 (right), 13, 14, 16, 26 (top & bottom right), 41, 42

Root Resources—© Jane H. Kriete, 6 (top); © Russell A. Kriete, 6 (bottom left); © Lewis Portnoy, 37 (right)

Society for Cultural Relations with the USSR—7, 11, 33

© Bob & Ira Spring—12 (left), 45 (top left & center left)

State Museums of the Moscow Kremlin, Photographed by Sheldan Collins, The Metropolitan Museum of Art—20

SuperStock International, Inc..—© Herb Levart, 45 (top right)

TSW/CLICK-Chicago—© Geoff Johnson, Cover; © Karen Sherlock, 44 (2 photos)

Worldwide Photos Specialty, Alexander M. Chabe—8, 10 (top), 19 (2 photos), 24, 30, 34 (2 photos), 37 (left), 39, 40, 43 (2 photos)

Len Meents—map on page 9

Cover—USSR, Moscow, Red Square, St. Basil's Cathedral

Library of Congress Cataloging-in-Publication Data

Jacobsen, Karen.
  The Soviet Union / by Karen Jacobsen.
    p.   cm. — (A New true book)
  Includes index.
  Summary: Describes the geography, history, people, and culture of the Soviet Union.
  ISBN 0-516-01109-X
  1. Soviet Union—Juvenile literature.
  [1. Soviet Union.] I. Title.
DK17.J24 1990   90-2177
947—dc20   CIP
                      AC

TABLE OF CONTENTS

The Nation...4

The Land...7

The European Plain and the Urals...11

Siberia...14

Soviet Central Asia...17

Early History...18

The Romanovs...23

Lenin and the Revolution...30

Joseph Stalin...32

The Iron Curtain and the Cold War...35

Life in the Soviet Union...37

Holidays and Recreation...41

Words You Should Know...46

Index...47

THE NATION

The Soviet Union is the largest nation in the world. Part of the Soviet Union is in Europe, but most of it is in Asia.

There are almost 290 million people in the Soviet Union. More than half of them are Russian. But there are over ninety other nationality groups in the Soviet Union. They speak more than fifty languages.

LATVIAN S.S.R. ESTONIAN S.S.R.
JANIAN
S.R.
o Tallinn
Riga
Vilna o
o Minsk
BELORUSSIAN S.S.R.
o Moscow

RUSSIAN S.F.S.R.

Kiev o
nev
UKRAINIAN S.S.R.
JAVIAN S.S.R.

GEORGIAN S.S.R.

Tbilisi
Yerevan
MENIAN
S.S.R.
RBAIJAN S.S.R.

Baku o

KAZAKH S.S.R.

UZBEK S.S.R.

TURKMEN S.S.R.

Ashkhabad
Tashkent

Alma-Ata

REPUBLICS OF THE SOVIET UNION

Frunze

Dushanbe

TADZHIK S.S.R.

KIRGHIZ S.S.R.

From west to east, the Soviet Union stretches more than 6,000 miles. It measures 3,200 miles from north to south.

The Soviet Union has
fifteen republics. Each
republic is governed by a
soviet—a council of elected
members.

The Soviet Union also has
a central government. Its

5

Above: A view of Moscow, the capital city of the Soviet Union. Interior (left) and the exterior (below at right) of the GUM department store on Red Square in Moscow.

headquarters are in the capital city of Moscow.

THE LAND

The northernmost part of the Soviet Union is an icy, flat land called the tundra. It stretches all along the Arctic Ocean.

South of the tundra is the taiga, a thick forest that

Most of the trees in the taiga are needle-leaf evergreens.

grows on swampy ground. The ground of the taiga thaws in summer and freezes in winter.

South of the taiga are flat, grass-covered plains called the steppe. On the steppe, the summer lasts long enough for crops to grow.

A wheat field on the steppe after the harvest

The six land regions of the Soviet Union are: the European Plain, the Ural Mountains, the West Siberian Plain, the Central Siberian Plateau, the East Siberian Uplands, and Soviet Central Asia.

South of the steppe is the desert. It has little rainfall and is very dry.

The Soviet Union has six land regions. Each region is defined by the mountains or rivers that form its natural borders.

9

Kiev (above), lies on both sides of the Dnieper River. Leningrad (below) is built on a series of islands connected by bridges.

Fishing for sturgeon in the Volga River. The eggs of the sturgeon are used to make a special food called caviar.

THE EUROPEAN PLAIN AND THE URALS

Nearly three-fourths of the Soviet people live on the European Plain. It has most of the nation's best farmland and its three largest cities— Moscow, Leningrad, and Kiev.

The Volga River and many other streams and rivers run through the European Plain.

11

Some roads cross the rugged Caucasus Mountains,
but railroads must go around them.

The Caucasus Mountains
lie between the Black Sea
and the Caspian Sea. They
mark the southern edge of
the European Plain.

The Ural Mountains divide
the European Plain from Siberia.

The Urals hold large deposits of iron, manganese, nickel, and copper ores. They also have vast supplies of oil and natural gas. Refineries and factories built near these resources provide jobs and products for many Soviet people.

Workers building a pipeline battle the severe winters of Siberia.

13

Wooden houses in a town in Siberia

SIBERIA

All the land east of the
Urals is known as Siberia.
Much of the West Siberian
Plain is not good for farming.
In the far north the tundra is

frozen all year round. In the taiga, the land is very marshy. On the steppe, Soviet farmers graze cattle and grow potatoes, beets, and grain crops.

The Central Siberian Plateau starts as lowland in the north. But, in the south, the Central Plateau ends in the high slopes of the Sayan and Baikal mountains. The Central Plateau is a major coal-mining area.

Ice and snow cover most of Siberia for six months of the year.
The temperature sometimes drops to ninety degrees below zero.

Eastern Siberia is a land
of high mountains, plateaus,
and valleys. For most of the
year, the region is very cold.
But for a short time in the
summer, the Lena River
thaws and flows into the
Arctic Ocean.

SOVIET CENTRAL ASIA

Soviet Central Asia is unlike the rest of the Soviet Union. It is much warmer and the land is mainly flat and low. In some areas, the land is below sea level. The Karagiye Depression, near the Caspian Sea, dips to 433 feet below sea level.

Soviet Central Asia has no tundra, taiga, or steppe. It is best known for its deserts called *kums*. The Kara Kum has black sands and the Kyzyl Kum has red sands.

EARLY HISTORY

Long ago, the land that is now the Soviet Union was mainly wilderness. In the Asian part, small tribes of hunters lived in the taiga or on the tundra. In the European part, the people were hunters and farmers. They lived in small villages built near rivers.

In the A.D. 800s, Vikings from Scandinavia sailed down the rivers. They captured the villages and

Left: Vladimir I brought Christianity to Kiev. Right: The remains of the Golden Gate of Kiev, which was built in the 1000s.

took the land. Some historians say the Vikings were called Rus. The land controlled by the Rus became known as Russia.

In 988, Vladimir I was the ruler of the city of Kiev. He became a Christian and joined the Greek Orthodox

This old manuscript is written in Cyrillic, the name for the Russian alphabet.

Church. Vladimir brought the Greek alphabet, reading, and writing to the Russian people. Later, Russians used the Greek letters as a basis for the Russian alphabet.

In 1237, Russia was invaded from the east by a

The Mongols, who were famous horsemen, came from the lands north of China. They conquered a huge empire in Asia.

Mongol army. The Mongols controlled parts of Russia for more than 200 years.

In 1462, Ivan III captured the land around Moscow and became king. Ivan III was the first Russian ruler to call himself czar.

Ivan IV was a cruel ruler. He killed his own son during a fit of anger.

In 1547, Ivan IV—known as Ivan the Terrible—became czar. He took over land by force. Ivan IV made a law that serfs, the people who worked the land, were the property of the landowners. Under the new law, serfs could be bought and sold like slaves.

THE ROMANOVS

After the death of Ivan IV, Russia was without a strong leader. In 1613, the Russian leaders chose Michael Romanov, a sixteen-year-old boy, to be the new czar. The Romanov family ruled Russia for the next 300 years.

In 1689, Michael's grandson became Czar Peter. Peter changed his backward country into a European power.

In 1697 and 1698, Peter traveled to western Europe.

Czar Peter is known as Peter the Great
because of his work in modernizing Russia.

He studied shipbuilding,
architecture, and trade. Then
he brought these skills back
to Russia and taught them to
Russian workers.

He built ships and created

a Russian navy. He built factories and schools.

In 1703, Czar Peter started to build a new capital, St. Petersburg (now Leningrad), near the Baltic Sea.

In 1762, Catherine II became czarina. She ruled

Peter and his successors brought French and Italian architects to Russia to design palaces and gardens. This view is from Peter's summer palace at Petrodvorets.

Catherine the Great (above) encouraged the performance of opera (top right) and orchestral music (bottom) in Russia.

until 1796. During her reign, the Russian army captured land from Poland and from the Ottoman Empire (now Turkey). Catherine made Russia a center for the arts.

In 1812, Napoleon invaded Russia. But during the fierce Russian winter, the French were forced to retreat to France.

In 1861, Czar Alexander II decided to make reforms. He freed the serfs and gave them small pieces of land. He set up local governments.

But many Russians thought the reforms were not enough. They wanted to end the power of the czar. In 1881, terrorists assassinated Alexander II.

Left: Czar Nicholas II. Right: United States president Theodore Roosevelt (at center) helped negotiate the end of the war between Japan and Russia in 1905.

In 1894, Nicholas II became czar. In 1904, Russia went to war with Japan. The Japanese won. Thousands of Russians were killed or wounded.

After the war, there were strikes and protest marches. The protesters wanted the czar to give up his throne.

Russian soldiers march off to fight in World War I.

Many strikers were killed by the czar's police.

In 1914, Russia entered World War I on the side of Great Britain and France. Millions of Russian soldiers were killed or wounded fighting the Germans and Austrians. Nicholas became even more unpopular.

LENIN AND THE REVOLUTION

Lenin speaks to Communist troops in Moscow's Red Square in May 1919.

In March 1917, a revolution began in Moscow and St. Petersburg. Czar Nicholas was forced to give up the throne of Russia. He and his family were executed in 1918. In October 1917, Communist Bolsheviks led by Vladimir Ilyich Ulyanov, known as Lenin, seized power.

In March 1918, although

the war in Europe was still going on, Lenin signed a peace treaty with Germany.

Inside Russia there was a civil war between the Communists and the Whites. The Whites hated the Communists and wanted a new czar to lead Russia. The bitter civil war lasted from 1918 until 1920, when the Communists won.

In 1922, Lenin and his comrades formed a new nation called the Union of Soviet Socialist Republics.

JOSEPH STALIN

In 1924, Lenin died. Joseph Stalin took over. Millions of people who disagreed with Stalin were killed or sent to prison in Siberia.

Stalin set up Five-Year Plans to modernize farming and industry in the Soviet Union. Many small farms were joined together to make large farms controlled by the government. Factory

Joseph Stalin became a powerful dictator in the Soviet Union. He had more power than a czar.

workers shared the profits made by their factory.

In 1939, Stalin made a secret treaty with Adolf Hitler and Nazi Germany. Germany promised to give Estonia, Latvia, Lithuania, part of Poland, and half of Finland to the Soviet Union.

In return, the Soviet Union agreed not to fight against the Germans in World War II. But, in 1941, the German armies invaded the Soviet Union, and Stalin then entered the war on the side of the United States and Great Britain.

During World War II, the Germans fought the Russians at Leningrad. German planes (left) bombed the city. Russian guns (right) held back the German troops for over two years.

THE IRON CURTAIN
AND THE COLD WAR

After World War II ended
in 1945, the Soviet Union
took control of Estonia,
Latvia, and Lithuania. Also,
many other countries—
Poland, East Germany,
Czechoslovakia, Hungary,
Romania, Yugoslavia,
Bulgaria, and Albania—
became Communist
countries.

During the 1950s, 1960s,
and 1970s, the Soviet Union
and the United States were

enemies. Both sides were prepared for war. This state of mutual distrust was called the Cold War. Many times during those years, events came close to turning the Cold War into a "hot war."

In the 1980s, the Soviet Union, headed by Mikhail Gorbachev, began to change. Communism wasn't working. The Soviet republics were given more freedom. Poland, Hungary, and other European Communist countries held free elections.

Musicians (left) play banduras, popular folk musical instruments. Russian dancers (right) opened the Moscow Summer Olympics in 1980.

LIFE IN THE SOVIET UNION

By the late 1800s, Russia had its own master performers in the arts. Russian musicians, dancers, and singers thrilled audiences in other European countries.

The Communists kept the training schools and theaters open.

Before the Russian Revolution, three-quarters of the Russian people could not read or write. Today, 99 percent of the Soviet people are literate.

Most Soviet students attend school for eleven years.

Students in the first four grades study art, language, music, arithmetic, nature, and Soviet history. In the fifth through eighth grades, students study algebra, geometry, physics, zoology, anatomy, and literature.

An English
class in
Leningrad

Some students in the ninth through eleventh grades attend special schools to prepare them for jobs. They may take courses in engineering, agriculture, or industry.

Other students attend general secondary schools. They prepare to study

Students at
Tbilisi State
University
in the Soviet
republic of Georgia

advanced sciences or languages in a university.

Communism does not approve of religion, but some people do practice their religion in the Soviet Union. There are Russian Orthodox Christians, Muslims, Roman Catholics, Jews, Buddhists, and other religious groups.

HOLIDAYS AND RECREATION

In old Russia, Christian holy days such as Christmas and Easter were very important. Today, in the Soviet Union, New Year's Day is celebrated with special foods, gift giving, and a visit from Grandfather Frost.

Grandfather Frost and Lady Snow are represented in New Year's Day celebrations in the Soviet Union.

Other special days are
May Day—International
Labor Day—on May 1, and
November 7, the anniversary
of the Communist Revolution.
Soviet athletes excel in
swimming and diving, as
well as in gymnastics, track

Soviet children start early to train for sports such as gymnastics.

Young chess players (left) take notes on the game.
Students learn archery (right) in the republic of Georgia.

and field, and skiing. Soccer
is the most popular sport,
but hockey is also a favorite.

Soviets of all ages love to
play chess. Many Soviet
families go hiking and
camping on their summer
vacation.

43

With the reform of Communism, the many peoples of the Soviet Union (right and opposite page) are hopeful that the future will bring greater freedom and a higher standard of living.

The Soviet Union is a beautiful and powerful country. Its proud people have faced many problems — wars, shortages, and a bitter cold climate. But always they have held on to life and found ways to enjoy it. Most Soviet people hope that life in the 1990s will be better than ever before.

WORDS YOU SHOULD KNOW

civil war (SIH • vil WOR) — a war between two groups in the same country

comrades (KAHM • radz) — friends; partners

czar (ZAR) — the title used by the rulers of Russia; means "caesar" in Russian

dictator (DIK • tay • ter) — single ruler who has absolute power over the people of a country

kum (KUM) — a desert

literate (LIH • ter • it) — able to read and write

marshy (MAR • shee) — having ground covered by shallow water

Mongols (MAHNG • gilz) — a people from the area north of China who conquered a large empire in Asia

Ottoman Empire (OT • oh • man EM • pyre) — empire of the Ottoman Turks in Turkey and the eastern Mediterranean that lasted from about 1300 to 1922

plateau (PLAT • oh) — an area of elevated flat land

refineries (rih • FYN • er • eez) — plants where crude oil is made into products such as gasoline and heating oil

republic (rih • PUB • lik) — a country with elected leaders

serf (SERF) — a farm worker who could be sold along with the land

soviet (SOH • vee • eht) — a governing council consisting of elected members

steppe (STEP) — broad, level grassland

taiga (TY • gah) — forest made up mostly of needle-leaf evergreen trees

terrorists (TAIR • er • ists) — people who use violent methods to bring about political change

tundra (TUHN • dra) — cold, treeless lands near the Arctic Ocean

Vikings (VY • kings) — raiders from Scandinavia who overran much of western and northwestern Europe

INDEX

Albania, 35
Alexander II, 27
Arctic Ocean, 7, 16
arts, 26, 37
Asia, 4, 18
Austrians, 29
Baikal Mountains, 15
Baltic Sea, 25
Black Sea, 12
Bolsheviks, 30
Bulgaria, 35
Caspian Sea, 12, 17
Catherine II, 25-26
Caucasus Mountains, 12
Central Siberian Plateau, 15
civil war, 31
Cold War, 36
Communists and communism,
    30, 31, 35, 36, 37, 40
czars, 21, 22, 23, 24, 25, 26, 27,
    28, 29, 31
Czechoslovakia, 35
desert, 9
Eastern Siberia, 16
East Germany, 35
education, 38-40
Estonia, 33, 35
Europe, 4, 18, 23, 24, 31, 37
European Plain, 11-12
factories, 13, 25, 32-33
farming, 8, 11, 14, 15, 17, 32
Finland, 33

Five-Year Plans, 32
forests, 7
France, 27, 29
Germany and Germans, 29, 31,
    33, 34
Gorbachev, Mikhail, 36
government, 5, 6, 27
Great Britain, 29, 34
Greek alphabet, 20
Greek Orthodox Church, 19-20
Hitler, Adolf, 33
holidays, 41
Hungary, 35, 36
Ivan III, 21
Ivan IV, 22, 23
Japan, 28
Karagiye Depression, 17
Kara Kum, 17
Kiev, 11, 19
kums, 17
Kyzyl Kum, 17
landowners, 22
land regions, 9
languages, 4
Latvia, 33, 35
Lena River, 16
Lenin (Vladimir Ilyich Ulyanov),
    30, 31, 32
Leningrad, 11
Lithuania, 33, 35
minerals and mining, 13, 15
Mongols, 21

Moscow, 6, 11, 21, 30
mountains, 9, 12, 15, 16
Napoleon, 27
nationality groups, 4
natural gas, 13
navy, 24-25
Nicholas II, 28, 29, 30
oil, 13
Ottoman Empire, 26
people, 4, 11, 38
Peter (czar), 23-24
Poland, 26, 33, 35, 36
reading, 20, 38
refineries, 13
reforms, 27
religion, 40
republics, Soviet, 5, 36
resources, 13
revolution, 30, 38
rivers, 9, 11, 18
Romania, 35
Romanov, Michael, 23
Romanovs, 23-29, 30
Rus, 19
Russian alphabet, 20
St. Petersburg (Leningrad), 25, 30

Sanyan Mountains, 15
Scandinavia, 18
serfs, 22, 27
Siberia, 12, 14-16, 32
Soviet Central Asia, 17
soviets, 5
sports and recreation, 42-43
Stalin, Joseph, 32, 33, 34
steppe, 8, 9, 15, 17
strikes, 28, 29
taiga, 7-8, 15, 17, 18
tundra, 7, 14, 17, 18
Union of Soviet Socialist
    Republics, 31
United States, 34, 35
Ural Mountains, 12, 13, 14
Vikings, 18-19
Vladimir I, 19
Volga River, 11
West Siberian Plain, 14-15
Whites, 31
World War I, 29
World War II, 34, 35
writing, 20, 38
Yugoslavia, 35

About the Author

Karen Jacobsen is a graduate of the University of Connecticut and Syracuse University. She has been a teacher and is a writer. She likes to find out about interesting subjects and then write about them.